ADJUSTMENT OF SENIOR CITIZENS

ADJUSTMENT OF SENIOR CITIZENS

By

Ms. T.Indira Rani

M.A., M.Ed.

Lecturer in English

B.R. College of Education

Guntur – 522 002, (A.P.)

Editors

Dr. B.Vijaya Kumari

M.Sc., M.Ed., M.Phil., Ph.D.

Vice-Principal

A.L. College of Education

Guntur – 522 002 (A.P.)

Dr. D. Ramesh

M.A., M.A., (Ph.D)

Asstt. Professor

Deptt. of Anthropology

Andhra University

Visakhapatnam – 530 003 (A.P.)

&

Dr. T.J.Mouni Suvarna Raju

M.A., M.Ed., Ph.D.

Principal

K.P.N. College of Education

Gantyada, Vizianagaram Distt. - 535 215, (A.P.)

DISCOVERY PUBLISHING HOUSE PVT. LTD.

NEW DELHI-110 002

Reprinted - 2019

First Published - 2010

ISBN: 978-81-8356-622-3

Adjustment of Senior Citizens

Published by:

DISCOVERY PUBLISHING HOUSE PVT. LTD.
4383/4B, Ansari Road, Darya Ganj
New Delhi-110 002 (India)
Phone: +91-11-23279245, 23253475; 43596065
E-mail: discoverybooksindia@gmail.com
discoverypublishinghouse@gmail.com
web: www.discoverypublishinggroup.com

Printed at:
Infinity Imaging Systems
Delhi

Dedicated
To the Senior Citizens

PROF. Y.F.W. PRASADA RAO,
Former Dean and Professor,
Department of Education,
Andhra University, Visakhapatnam, A.P.

And

PROF. V. PRAMEELA BOSE,
Former Dean and Professor,
Department of Psychology,
Andhra University, Visakhapatnam, A.P.

For recognizing their able and noble services to the fields of Education and Psychology

Preface

There are four major stages in a human being. They are childhood, adulthood, middle age and old age. Old age is the last and the individual face physiological and psychological problems at this stage. After crossing the age of sixty, they are treated as senior citizens of our country and they are dependent on seeking help of somebody especially on their grand children.

Majority of senior citizens were retired from the services and spend their time in a relaxed and peaceful atmosphere. Hence, they have to adjust with the living situations. If a person who is well adjusted to the environment can have an elongated life span.

The present study focused on the adjustment of senior citizens in some dimensions with some groups. Different types of adjustments were concluded in various situations.

This book will be useful to the Psychologists, Educational Psychologists, Counsellors, Educationists, Anthropologists and Researchers.

Dr. T.J.M.S. Raju

Contents

"As for the days of our life, they contain seventy years or if due to strength, eighty years yet their pride is, but labor and sorrow for soon it is gone and we fly away."

(Psalms 90th chapter 10th verse)

"The hoary head is a crown of glory, if it be found in the way of righteousness."

(Proverbs 16th chapter 31st verse)

1

The Problem and the Significance of the Study

Introduction

Ageing is a natural phenomenon common to all human beings. The last period of ageing is old age and ultimately it is a closing period. Generally we can consider age sixty, is the starting period of old age.

Chronologically after retirement, we can consider old age or retirement age, that is, the age of sixty. According to the norms of the State or Central governments, the old age people who cross age sixty are treated as senior citizens. The senior citizens are honoured by giving railway concessions, seats in buses, old age pensions, higher interest rates for fixed deposits etc. There is a quotation saying that *"Grey hair is respected"*.

According to Hindu mythology, *"Vridhatyam-Jarasa Vina"* which means, let the old age be without senility or disability (Poet Kalidasa, II century B.C.).

According to new American Standard Bible version, the Lord's Prophet named 'Moses' mentioned that:

> "As for the days of our life, they contain seventy years, or if due to strength, eighty years, yet their pride is, but labor and sorrow for soon it is gone and we fly away."
>
> (*Psalms* 90th chapter 10 verse).

If a man has a total life span of seventy years, among this period, a decade will be old age. If a man possesses high energy he will be having another decade more.

The high energy means, if a man obeys the rules and regulations of the government as well as God, then he can gain ten years more for his life span. The variations of age are according to the will of God.

After crossing sixty years of age, senile dementia will occur. It is the loss of cognitions. When the age increases slowly, the human potentialities such as remembering, reasoning, problem solving, memory, thinking, etc., will gradually decreases. So, even if a professor having high potentialities of knowledge, losses every thing in his old age.

During old age, the person has to become dependent on somebody. At the same time, he has to spend his life in lonely atmosphere. Sometimes, the older people are alone in their homes. So, there is a lot of variation between his worked conditions, in relationship with retirement age or old age. Hence, the old person has to adjust himself, to the environmental dimensions. A proper adjustment will make him a better and comfortable life. An improper adjustment will lead him a problematic life.

Conceptual Background

The study of behavior of ageing is known as "Gerontology". Now-a-day's, many studies are conducted in the aspects of ageing. The life span of human being is also increasing, because of various studies of gerontology.

The age along with adjustment with new situations, is an important factor to lead a comfortable life. So that, the present study focus on so many aspects of ageing factors, along with various dimensions of adjustment.

Meaning of Adjustment

Many psychologists, sociologists, environmentalists, biologists' defined adjustment in many ways.

Biologists' defined adjustment as 'adaptation' or 'accommodation'. *Even, a small animal like Amoeba, which is a unicellular animal, if it finds any obstacle immediately, it back up and goes in another way.* It is a biological adaptation of smaller organisms. The larger animals such as tigers, lions etc., living in a jungle when kept in a zoo, the animals have to accommodate to the new environment otherwise, they may die. This is all about the biological adaptation of animals.

Sociologists also define adjustment as, an accommodation. People from one place to another place migrate, because of their livelihood or fear of wars or transfer of jobs or better placements in abroad etc. Some agriculturalists if they go for their seasonal jobs so that, they will stay up to a period of time in the working area and after completion; they will come back to their own place. Whenever a family or a group of people migrate from one place to other some new problems of existence, may arise so that, they have to accommodate themselves beyond those problems. Some tribal groups frequently change their places of stay. They will go in a group, so each member will perform some duty. Like wise, they will prepare food for whole group and they will enjoy in music or singing etc.

The environmentalists, also supports the term adjustment because of seasons and because of the variations of temperature in climate and also by natural calamities or hazards. Due to these events, many social relationships and contents may spoil, because of the damage of the communication systems and technologies. In small cold countries because of the winter season, they shift their head quarters from one place to other. In some other cold countries the sea beds and river beds will become as ground so that people play on the ice grounds, and the people of that country have to adjust according to their climatic conditions. Proper and good adjustment leads them healthy and with some precautions, they have to take for each climatic condition. Any how, people have to adjust according to the new environmental situations.

The above three adjustments are related to the outside or external factors but, the psychological adjustment is related to, both external as well as internal factors. A psychological adjustment is to maintain a harmonious relationship between the individual and the environment or the external factors. There are so many psychological aspects, inter mingled with the adjustment factors. Home adjustment, health adjustment, social adjustment etc. are all related to external environmental and individual factors where as the factors related to emotional aspects are inter-related with psychological as well as materialistic influence so that it is a psychological factor.

A proper adjustment is one, which the individual adjust within himself as well as, with the other situations of the environment. A well adjusted person leads his life in a smoother way where as, the person that does not adjusted properly will become a problem for him and also to the society. Now-a-day's, the world is giving importance to the materialistic things. The immaterialist things such as love, affection are gradually diminishing. So that, in this present situation every person has to lead independently without depending on others for any aspect.

The study mainly focused on aged and senior citizens of our country so that; it is the part of the researcher to emphasis the study in various dimensions of adjustment in relationship with the demographic variables. The study also elaborates various differences, based on the statistical calculations.

Old age is an ultimate stage for eternity. At this age, every young generation must look after their old parents in a careful way. But in west, they simply admit their parents in old age homes. Of course, the old age homes are also look after every citizen in a careful way. But they cannot receive love and affection that will obtain only in home. So, the present study also deals with the emotional balances and imbalances and also it will helpful for the younger generation as a message. The researcher has taken a relevant problem to study, and the problem has a significant importance in the educational system. The study also useful for other researchers related to gerontology, adjustment and other related dimensions.

Definitions

Many psychologists, sociologists, biologists and environmentalists defined adjustment. Some of the related definitions, are presented in this section.

- Good defined (1945) psychological adjustment as:
  - (*i*) Process of finding modes of behavior suitable to the environment or to change in the environment.

(*ii*) Biologically as a change or acquired characteristics in an organism, that enables it to meet the requirements of it environment.

- Shaffer (1952) defined adjustment as 'tension reduction'.
- According to Shaffer and Shoben (1956) "Life consists of a series of such sequences in which needs are aroused and satisfied. This family pattern is the process of adjustment.
- Shaffer (1956) defined the relationship, which becomes established among the biological heritage or organism, the environment and the personality is adjustment.
- Lindgren (1959) defined adjustment as the act or process of establishing a satisfactory psychological relationship between the individual and his environment.
- Smith (1961) defined a good adjustment as one, which is both realistic and satisfying. At least in the long run, it reduces to a minimum the frustrations, the tensions and anxieties, which a person must endure.
- Bhatia (1965) defined adjustment as an all-inclusive term meaning relationship between an individual and his environment through which his needs are satisfied in accordance with social demands.

Sources

The information related to various adjustments for my study, was collected from senicr citizens who are staying in some old age homes and some of the individual houses of urban area in Guntur town.

1.3 Need of the Present Study

John Keats's in one of his sonnets *"The Human Seasons"* compared the season with the stages of man.

'He has his winter too of pale misfeature,
Or else he would forego his mortal nature',

In the last stage, he compared the old age with that of the winter season. During winter, the climate is very cold and fog makes to shiver every human being. So old age is the final stage of man which is pale and energy.

Shakespeare in his poem *"All the world's a stage"* compares the world to a stage, dividing human life into seven stages.

> *'That ends this strange eventful history, is second childishness and more oblivion, sans teeth, sans eyes, sans taste, sans everything.'*

The last stage, old age is man's second childhood in which man becomes forgetful, losing his teeth, eyesight, taste and almost everything in life.

Likewise, American and British poets and so many poets emphasized and gave very much importance to old age. It is a perfect life circle of human being one cannot escape from this circle. Everyone has to experience with the system of old age.

The responsibilities of the old are fulfilled and it is the age of retirement so that, the person may live and lead in a calm and pleasant atmosphere in a pleasant environment.

Due to, so many changes of bio-chemistry during old age, so many physical changes takes place like, loosing of teeth, weakness, loss of eyesight, raise of blood pressure, sugar or diabetics etc., because of the physical defects, the person has to adjust with his health.

Due to the scientific and technological development in homes, so many new changes have made during the present environment also like, watching TV, hearing music, telephone, machinery usages in home, computer etc., are quiet new to the older people, so that they have to adjust in home in the present existing world.

In the past world, they lived a joint family system or complex family system so that, the people are very helpful when ever they are in trouble or need. So, the social climate is stronger than the past world. But in the present system, the nuclear family system arises and every person is living independently. Due to the independent life system, working situations and hectic schedules make him some social disturbances in their relationships. Likewise, older people also stay along with their children or else, some frequent changes from one place to another or else, they will admit to old age homes. In these situations, there is a place to study on the social relationships of the older people.

Generally in old age, the behaviour of a person may change. He cannot resist himself either physically or mentally. Some irritation, anger and tension may create harm to the older person, as well as harm to others also. So, older people have to adjust emotionally. Due to high emotional stress, leads even to death caused by B.P., over B.P. or heart attacks etc. So, the mental aspects of older persons must be calm and cool. They have to maintain balanced situations in every step of life.

Some educated older people, if they worked in government sector may get some pension so that, they can lead their life independently. In some families, unemployed youth or children are even depending on the older people for their financial aspects. For some older people, it is a good financial adjustment and for some it is a worst adjustment. What ever the situation may be the older people has to spend their money in a planned way so that, they will spend money for the food needs, hospital and medical needs for other necessities. So, the spending of expenditure is mainly based on the earning that the person receives. In this context, older persons have to adjust in money matters.

Due to all these factors in the present visible environment, there is a great need to focus the study on the dimensions of adjustment like home, social, health, financial ,emotional etc., so that, these are the major parts of dimensions of adjustment. The present study mainly focus on, various adjustment factors, based on their gender, the categorization of age, job holders or unemployed etc., are consider as the independent variables.

Based on theses factors, and based on the observations of the society, the gerontology is a present and current problem to study the dimensions and discuss various matters of the aged people. The study is quiet suitable for the present generation so that, every one has to experienced with the older people in their homes. So, it is a quiet justification to focus on the study of the aged people.

The Process of Adjustment

Human adjustment is a never ending process (Ruch, 1970). It starts right from the birth of the child and continues till his death. It does not stop at any time, rather it goes on with life.

Adjustment is a process by which, a living organism maintains balance between its needs and the circumstances, which influence the satisfaction of these needs. It is therefore, a state of harmony between the needs, activities, resources of a person and the condition of his milieu.

Lazarus (1976) states that, adjustment consists of, the psychological processes by means of which; the individual manages to cope with various demands or pressures. Thus, adjustment is concerned with values. One cannot think of adjustment without being, sensitive to the good and the bad or to the right and the wrong. Adjustment is that, which brings to a person and to his social groups the good, and protects him from the bad.

The Characteristics of Old Age People

The characteristics are categorized into physical and mental characteristics.

Physical Characteristics:

- *Weakness:* During old age, the body becomes weak so that, older persons can not do too much work.
- *Loss of vision:* Older people gradually losses vision. They must wear glasses for clear vision.
- *Loss of teeth:* During old age, the older person losses his teeth.
- *Arthritis:* Many older persons suffer with joint pains during old age.
- *Hair becomes grey:* All the hair becomes grey and white color.
- *Skin wrinkles:* Skin becomes wrinkled and it losses its elasticity.

Mental Characteristics:

- *Senile Dementia:* The older person losses the cognition, like thinking, reasoning, remembering etc.

- *Loss of appetite:* The older persons losses the memory and intelligence.
- *Loss of skills:* Even a skill worker, losses all his skills during old age. If a musician who plays melodious music by an instrument, can not play during old age.

Rationale

The topic what author has chosen, is the relevant topic from educational psychology background. There are so many branches of psychology among them. Gerontology is 'the study of the behaviour of the senior citizens'. Secondly, adjustment is also a broader topic, from the background of educational psychology. Adjustment is the harmonious relationship between the senior citizens, with that of his environment. So, both the terms in this title and the topic, what author has chosen is purely from educational psychology under educational field.

"Getting older is getting better"

—*Warnick*

"Old age is a period of decline"

The 21st Century is often called the "Age of ageing"

"And the honour of old men is their gray hair"

2

Review of Related Literature

Introduction

A thorough look was kept on various journals, magazines, educational reviews, previous published work etc., to catch some related literature from Indian and foreign studies based on senior citizens adjustment.

Observations

The following observations were made in the review of literature related to Indian and foreign studies.

Indian Studies

(1) Title : 'Elderly and their counselling needs'.

Researcher : Kapur Pramilla, (1994).

Findings : Her results declare that,

(*i*) Health and financial problems are the major areas in which the elderly have needs and face problems so that, they have require help.

(*ii*) Other finding revealed that, the economic problem is a serious problem as 40.6% and 13.8% elderly in urban and rural areas are economically dependent. Due to economic difficulty, respondent reported sadness and frustration.

(*iii*) And the last finding showed that, poor economic conditions along with age may exert pressure and give rise to problems to the aged. Usually, they are over demanding and have too many expectations from their children who also work very hard.

(2) Title : 'Extra familial rehabilitation and conditions of the institutionalized elderly people'

Researcher: Khan (1997).

Findings :

(*i*) *Gender*: The findings conducted that, gender placed an important role that, the number of women is greater than that of the men in age groups 60 to 64, while the number of men is higher in the aged groups of 65 to 69 years.

(*ii*) *House Hold:* The house hold work like most elderly people live in larger families that is, 5 to 8 members and 22% elderly individuals live in smaller families consisting of 3 to 4 members.

(*iii*) *Economic Activities:* In the aspect of economic activities, the elderly belonging to agricultural families contribute in the various stages of cultivation. It was observed that, the elderly constitute an important and productive component sharing socio economic duties and tests essential for the family and community.

(3) Title : 'Stress and coping styles among the oldest-old'

Researchers: Uma Devi, T, Sudha Rani, N.N and Jumuna, D (2002).

Findings : Their results indicate that, through stressful life events are common for many of the impact of stress and type of coping was related to social supports, gender, self perception of health, life out look and value orientation.

(4) Title : 'Elderly widows in old age homes'.

Researcher : Kundal Agarwal (2002).

Findings :

(*i*) The findings conducted that, major of elderly widows in old age homes is the result of non-adjustment with their family members and due to a feeling of unwanted ness at home.

(*ii*) Another finding showed that, economic dependence is also one of the major causes of their neglect at home. 10% respondents live at their own cost with the support of their children. Sixty per cent depend on old age homes. Thirty per cent elderly widows meet their needs with the help of fellow inmates and voluntary welfare organization.

(*iii*) And the last finding conducted that, all the respondents have adjusted with old age home life in a feeling of loneliness.

(5) Title : 'Problems of senior citizens in Guntur district.'

Researcher : Hima Bindu, K (2004)

Findings : The results explained that:

(*i*) The problems are due to their poor health, emotional insecurity, social withdrawal and non-adjustment. Senior citizens have more health problems compared to other problems.

(*ii*) The problems of senior citizens in free homes are more, when compare to paid and own houses due to economic insecurity and unwantedness by the family. Elderly men have more problems than elderly women.

(*iii*) The problems are the same in both small and large families. Very low income is also one of the causes for the problems of the senior citizens.

(6) Title : 'Intergenerational family support for older men and women in south India'.

Researchers: Sudha, S, Hrudaya Rajan, S, and Sharma, P.S. (2004).

Findings : The results declare that:

(*i*) Those that are widowed have more economic assets, male are more likely to live with children contrary to expectation and against the need based familial relationship model, older persons appear less likely to live with children.

(*ii*) Compared to those not working in any other occupation are more likely to live with children. Those who have more sons and daughters are more likely to live with children.

(*iii*) Most health related factors are not associated with the likely hood of co-residence, how ever reporting feeling in positive health is associated with a greater chance of living with children.

(7) Title : 'Grand Mothers: Needed or Avoided'.

Researcher : Archana Kaushik Panda (2004).

Findings : The results show that:

(*i*) Activities performed by the grand mothers for their grand children are independent of socio demographic variables like age, marital status, educational level and occupational status.

(*ii*) Even poor health conditions do not interfere sharing of activities with grand children. However, there is strong relation between psychological variables like loneliness, worry and tension, life satisfaction willingness to take up child care activities.

(*iii*) There were also aged women who have greater adjustment activities often willingly perform child care activities and they often enjoy love and respect of their family members.

(8) Title : 'Life styles of senior citizens.

Researcher : Beulah Hana Justina G. (2006).

Findings : Results indicated that,

(*i*) The people seem to have no time either for their parents in their mad rush to earn and make life more comfortable. They are sacrificing their familial duties.

(*ii*) We find the children's are the crèches and the aged or in the old age homes. We need to take care of them and drawn from their experience.

Foreign Studies

(1) Title : 'Senior citizens'

Researchers: Palmore and Lucikart, (1972), Edwards and

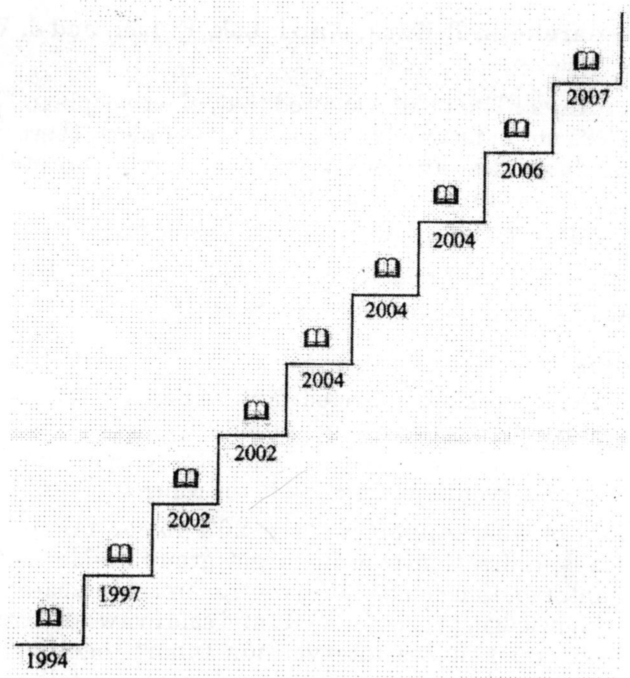

Indian related studies in year-wise order

klemmark, (1973), Spreitzer and Synder, (1974), Tornstan, (1975), Medley, (1976) and Markides and Martin, (1979).

Findings : The results revealed that, good health in later years is both directly and indirectly related to life satisfaction. Those who have seemed readily poor health were less common among older women than among men.

(2) Title : 'Study on aged persons'.

Researchers: Reid and Zeigur, (1997).

Findings : The finding shows that, health adjustment and problems of health appear to be one of the major concerns among the older people. Increasing age is accompanied by decreasing bodily resistance to illness. The psychological stresses supplement the suffering.

(3) Title : 'Attitudes of old people towards old age homes in Hong Kong'.

Researchers: T. Kwok, J.K.H. Luk, E. Lau, and J. Woo, (1997).

Findings : The results showed that, older people in Hong Kong were not in favor of an old age homes unless; there were physical disabilities and lack of family support. They are how ever, vulnerable to external pressures.

(4) Title : 'Older people can stay on their feet'

Researchers: Anne Kempton, Eric Van Beurden, Tim Sladden, Everald Garner and John Beard, (2000).

Findings :

(*i*) The results are collected from community based falls prevention programmed. At follow up there was a 22% non-significant lower incidence of self reported falls in the intervention compared to the control cohort.

(*ii*) This was supported by a 20% lower fall-related hospitalization rate in target group residents from intervention compared to control areas. Increased falls knowledge, physical activity and safe footwear were also observed in the intervention cohort together with improved balance and reduced intake of fall-related medications.

(5) Title : 'Retired and making a fresh start: Older Russian Immigrants discuss their adjustment in Israel'.

Researcher: Larissa Remennick (2003).

Findings :

(*i*) The findings indicate that, older immigrants have developed multiple ways for meaningful identification with Israel and generally perceived their resettlement experience as difficult but positive.

(*ii*) As their social net works were limited to the Russian Immigrant-community, most elders did not see their poor knowledge of Hebrew as a major integration obstacle.

(*iii*) The main reported difficulties were in the areas of housing, low income and weakening with younger family members.

(6) Title : Social support and psychological adjustment among Latin's with Arthritis: A test of a Theoretical Model.

Researcher : Ana.F. Abraido Lanza, (2004).

Findings :

(*i*) The result shows that social and cultural norms concerning the types of supported that are helpful and appropriate from specific support provided.

(*ii*) His study contributes to scarce literatures on the mechanisms that mediate the relationship between social support and adjustment, as well as illness and psychosocial adaptation among Latina women with chronic illness.

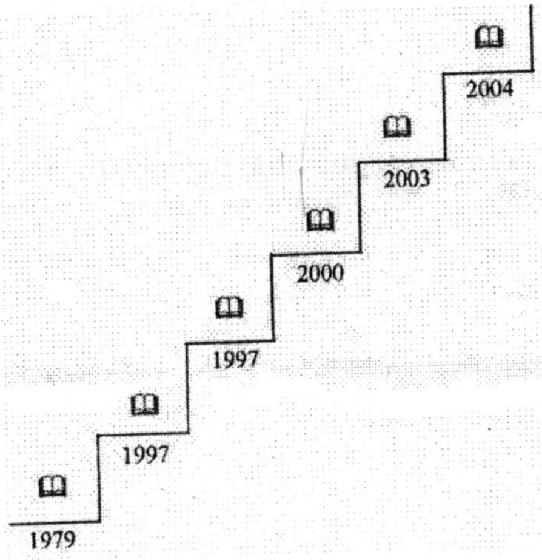

Foreign related studies in year-wise order

Perception of gaps and linkage to the present study

The previous studies based on the age factor, health factor, financial aspects, life styles, some problems related to medical aspects. But my study includes pensioners/non-pensioners dimension. It is a new concept and it is not present in previous study. So, the dimension of pensioners/non-pensioners is a linkage between the older person and the financial adjustment. Apart from these dimensions, the other adjustment factors like home adjustment, health adjustment, social adjustment, emotional adjustment and financial aspects. So my study will become a new adjustment study for the older people with some new dimensions.

"Ageing is a natural phenomenon, common to all living beings"

There is a popular saying about older people "use it or lose it"

There is a quotation saying that "Grey hair is respected".

3

The Research Procedure

Introduction

Research is a systematic procedure to identify a solution for the problem. It is the deviations from the actual events that are observed and collected from the old age people.

The researcher used survey method to collect data from old people in Guntur town. Some people are educated and some people are illiterates. From educated, the data was directly collected and from illiterates I translated the items in regional language and collected the data.

The data collection is hectic and very risky but it is a challenging task. So, many experiences were tasted in the real life situation. At the same time, I also observed many real life situations of old people in my personal interviews with them.

Author collected the data randomly so that, every subject has an equal importance in testing and collecting the data. Author collected the data from Guntur town houses and some old age homes.

The Statement of the Problem

The purpose of the investigation is, to study the senior citizens adjustment, in relation to home, health, society, emotional and financial adjustments in Guntur town.

This study attains to identify and compare the adjustment problems of male and female, 60-69 and 70 & above age groups and pensioners and non-pensioner senior citizens of Guntur Town.

The senior citizens asked to give positive and negative responses in different areas of the tool.

Objectives of the Study

1. To study the difference between the adjustments of the aged people, based on their gender.
2. To verify the adjustment of the aged people basing on the categorization of, 60-69 years and 70 & above years.
3. To study the difference between the pensioners and non-pensioner senior citizens.
4. To study the home adjustment among the aged.
5. To study the health adjustment among the aged.
6. To analyzé the social adjustment among the aged.
7. To investigate the emotional adjustment among the aged.
8. To verify the financial adjustment among the aged.

Hypotheses of the Study

1. Male senior citizens differ significantly from female senior citizens with respect to their home, health, social, emotional and financial adjustments.
2. 60-69 yr of age group senior citizens differ significantly when compare with 70-79 above yr of senior citizens with respect to home, health, social, emotional and financial adjustments.
3. Pension influences home, health, social, emotional and financial adjustments of senior citizens when compare with non-pensioner senior citizens.

The Variables

The following independent and dependent variables have been selected for my study.

Table 3.1

Sl.No	*Independent variables*	*Sl.No*	*Dependent variables*
1.	Gender: (a) Male (b) Female	1. 2. 3.	Home Adjustment Health Adjustment Social Adjustment

2. Age: (a) 60- 69 yrs (b) 70& above yrs 3. Financial Support (a) Pensioners (b) Non-Pensioners	4. Emotional Adjustment 5. Financial Adjustment

The Operational Definitions

- ***Senior Citizens:*** Senior citizens are the elderly citizens whose age is above 60 years.
- ***Old age:*** Old age is considered as a retirement age. In some occasions old age is considered as, a person needs rest. Old age is an age of unable to work.

  For the purpose of the study the researcher has categorized the age factor into lower age group and higher age group. The lower age group consists of the age between 60-69 yr and the higher age group 70 yr & above.
- ***Gender:*** Gender is segregation between men and women. It is the differentiation of sex that is male and female. Gender plays an important role in the research study because; it plays two different roles in society.
- ***Financial Support:*** Pension is an incentive given by the industry or government so that, the personnel had worked hard during young in the development of the firm so that, the firm has to given some financial help during his old age. A bonus or financial help given by the government after retirement of the service.
- ***Home Adjustment:*** The role performed by the senior citizens in a positive way in his home is known as home adjustment. A well adjusted person makes his role in his home with others in a well adjusted manner.
- ***Health Adjustment:*** So many physical as well as mental problems arise in old age. So, it is the role to perform to cope up the health of the senior citizens physically and mentally is known as health adjustment.
- ***Social Adjustment:*** The relationship of senior citizens with other members of community or group or society or family is known as social adjustment.

- ***Emotional Adjustment:*** There are some positive emotions and there are some negative emotions. The positive emotions should be performed by the senior citizens at the same time the balanced situation of negative emotions is known as emotional adjustment.
- ***Financial Adjustment:*** The management, expenditure and spending of money in a planned way by senior citizens is known as financial adjustment.

The Sample and Sampling Techniques

Table 3.2

Sl.No	*Old Age Homes*	*Sl..No*	*Individual Houses*
1.	Nirmal Hruday	1.	Naidupet
2.	Lydia home for the aged	2.	Hanumaiah Nagar
3.	Prema Hruday	3.	Bharathpet
		4.	Mallikharjunapet
		5.	Chandraiah Nagar
		6.	Cobaldpet
		7.	Nehru Nagar

The present study consists of 100 samples of senior citizens of Guntur town. The major sample was collected from individual houses and some data was collected from old age homes. The sample was collected by adopting random sampling technique.

The Schematic diagrams show the distribution of the sample under study.

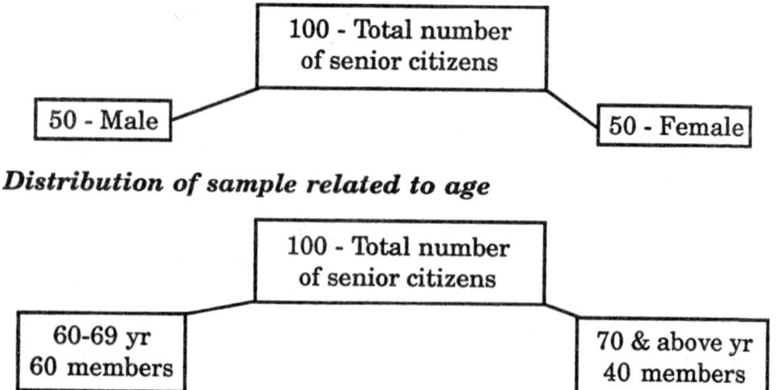

Distribution of sample with respect to pension

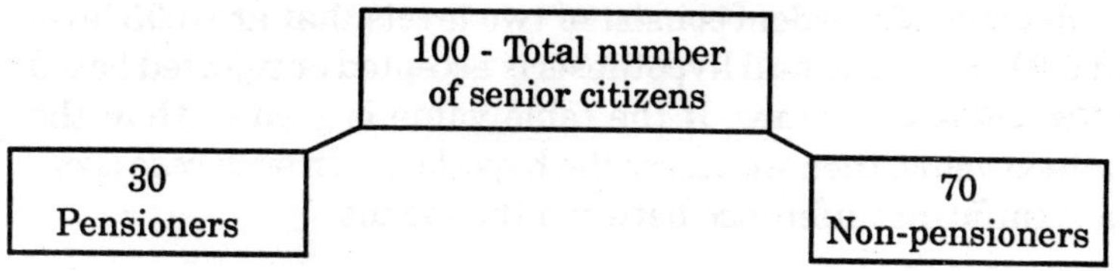

The Development of the Research Tool

The present research is aimed to know the opinions of adjustments of senior citizens, the tool taken is divided in to five parts namely A, B, C, D, E.

A total of 100 items were collected, and after analysis by experts in the research field, 75 items finally selected by eliminating 25 ambiguous items.

The following are the parts of the tool:

Part—A : Home adjustment (1-15)

Part—B : Health adjustment (16-30)

Part—C : Social adjustment (31- 45)

Part—D : Emotional adjustment (45 - 60)

Part—E : Financial adjustment (61-75)

Under each dependent variable a set of questions were constructed and the senior citizens were asked to put tick mark against each statement for yes/no.

The Statistical Techniques

- ***Arithmetic mean:*** The mean scores computed variable wise for all the five areas.
- ***Standard deviation***: Standard deviations were calculated variable wise in all.
- ***Mean difference***: Mean differences were calculated between the means.
- ***Critical ratio:*** Critical ratio is to know the significant difference of mean scores of opinions for the different variables in all five areas were constructed.
- ***Graphs:*** Graphical presentations were made on the average scores.

The Levels of Significance

The degrees of freedom consist of two levels that are 0.05 level and 0.01 level. The null hypothesis is accepted or rejected based on the obtained values. If the table value is greater than the obtained value, then we accept the hypothesis .In such case there is a significant difference between the means.

Robert Havighurst (1972) suggested the developmental tasks of late life as adjustment to decreasing physical strength and health, to retirement and reduced income, etc.

A Japanese proverb says "Ageing begins when we stop learning". The saying "resting is rusting" also holds well in the mental sphere. This means that mental fitness is also a significant factor in ageing process.

4

Analysis and Interpretation of Data

Introduction

Analysis of data means, studying the data in a totalistic manner, in order to know, the difficult task into a simpler derivation. In order to do such type of facts the verbal parts of material should be converted into numerical values.

The researcher has followed the under mentioned analysis to the data:

1. To observe the statement of the problem and its objectives.
2. To compute the data in various relevant statistical measurements.
3. To show the significant tables from the out put.
4. To make graphical representations of the deliberations.

The interpretations were noted, which are the essence of the results and critical points for the follow up study, for other investigations.

Acceptance of Opinions

In order to know the acceptance of the opinions, of senior citizens, towards each of the areas, in the dimensions of adjustment, have been calculated and are presented in the following tables.

Part – A: Home Adjustment

Table 4.1. Area of Home Adjustment

Sl.No	*Items*	*%*
1.	Do you feel happy at your home?	86
2.	Do you feel more comfortable at your home with out any disturbances?	87
3.	Do you look after your own things with out others support at your home?	81
4.	Do you concentrate on religious aspects like praying in your home?	85
5.	Do you feel lonely when you are alone at home?	33
6.	Do you spend some time by reading Holy Books?	54
7.	Do you spend some time in reading news paper or magazines at your home?	46
8.	Do you enjoy the leisure time by watching T.V?	39
9.	Do you enjoy favorable music at your home?	45
10.	Do you spend some time in gardening work at your home?	60
11.	Do you enjoy with your grand children at home?	77
12.	Do you satisfy with care and affection shown by your family members?	80
13.	Do others friends or relatives of your age will visit you at home?	69
14.	Do you spend some time in letter correspondence at your home?	48
15.	Do you feel secure with strangers when you are at home?	80

In the above table, the percentage represents the number of senior citizens, who expressed accepted opinion, towards that particular item in the area of home adjustment.

Part – B: Health Adjustment

Table 4.2. Area of Health Adjustment

Sl.No	*Items*	*%*
16.	Do you feel happy with your health?	80
17.	Do you have any problem with your sight?	72
18.	Do you suffer from joint pains?	59
19.	Do you usually feel exhausted?	59
20.	Are you usually anxious about your health?	64
21.	Do you take any care for your diet?	46
22.	Do you feel difficult at sleeping during nights?	70
23.	Do you keep on changing sides for a long time while lying on bed?	68
24.	Do you suffer from B.P?	62
25.	Do you suffer from sugar?	61
26.	Do you use long medication?	63
27.	Do you visit doctor regularly?	69
28.	Do you smoke?	85
29.	Do you take any alcohol?	86
30.	Are you doing walking exercises?	53

In the above table, the percentage represents the number of senior citizens, who expressed favorable opinion, towards that particular item in the area of health adjustment.

Part - C: Social Adjustment

Table 4.3. Area of Social Adjustment

Sl.No	*Items*	*%*
31.	Do you spend with your grand children?	81
32.	Do you share your pervious experiences with your children/grand children when ever necessary?	80
33.	Do you maintain friendly relationship with all?	90
34.	Do you usually get irritated on the members of your family?	82

...(Contd.)

Sl.No	*Items*	*%*
35.	Do you usually have trouble in recognizing people?	78
36.	Do your friends or relatives will visit you?	77
37.	Do you visit your friends or relatives of their houses?	67
38.	Do you spend some time with your neighbors?	72
39.	Are you troubled when you have different opinions on others?	83
40.	Do your heart is hurt by the small things of others?	79
41.	Do people usually think you to be a useless man?	92
42.	Do you visit your religious society?	66
43.	Do you have any gathering for recreation in the evening?	58
44.	Do you visit your children homes far away or in abroad?	44
45.	Do you travel to visit pilgrimage?	48

In the above table, the percentage represents the number of senior citizens, who expressed favorable opinion, towards that particular item in the area of social adjustment.

Part – D: Emotional Adjustment

Table 4.4. Area of Emotional Adjustment

Sl.No	*Items*	*%*
46.	Do you feel happy with your children/ grandchildren?	80
47.	Do you take care of your children/grand children?	74
48.	Do you like your friends/relatives?	67
49.	Do you like the presence of your neighbors?	85
50.	Do you affectionate with others of your age?	94
51.	Do you feel any anxiety or tension?	76
52.	Do you get anger easily or quickly?	77
53.	Do you get excited soon?	73
54.	Do you cry very soon?	56

...(Contd.)

Sl.No	*Items*	*%*
55.	Are you often disturbed of the fearful dreams?	52
56.	Do you feel fear by seeing quarrel?	47
57.	Do you feel that some trouble is ahead?	75
58.	Do you keep on thinking about your past?	47
59.	Do you get irritated in your home?	54
60.	Do you get disturbed with your children/grand children?	49

In the above table, the percentage represents the number of senior citizens, who expressed favorable opinion, towards that particular item in the area of emotional adjustment.

Part - E: Financial Adjustment

Table 4.5. Area of Financial Adjustment

Sl.No	*Items*	*%*
61.	Do you get pension?	30
62.	Do you satisfy with the money you get?	83
63.	Do you get any money from business?	37
64.	Do you get money from fields/cattle?	27
65.	Do you get rent from your own house?	61
66.	Do you have any fixed deposits?	48
67.	Do you pay any income tax for your assets?	3
68.	Do you have any financial problems?	63
69.	Do you face any problem by your family members because of financial aspects?	74
70.	Do you take any loan from bank or others?	39
71.	Do you spend your money to your children/ grand children?	93
72.	Do you support any religious/social organization?	79
73.	Do you spend money in a planned way?	88
74.	Do you feel that the expenditure is more at your home?	71
75.	Do you repay the amounts which you have taken from others?	96

In the above table, the percentage represents the number of senior citizens, who expressed favorable opinion, towards that particular item in the area of financial adjustment.

Critical Ratio Values

Critical ratio values, for mean scores of senior citizens in the aspects of adjustments in different areas.

Part – A: Home Adjustment of Gender

Table 4.6

Sl.No	*Gender*	*N*	*A.M*	*S.D*	*M.D*	*C.R*
1.	Male	50	24.82	2.60	0.24	0.48
2.	Female	50	24.58	2.51		

The constructed value is 0.48 and the table value at 98 degrees of freedom is at 0.05 level is 1.98. Therefore, null hypothesis is accepted and alternative hypothesis is rejected. There is no significant difference of opinion between male and female senior citizens regarding home adjustment problem.

Home Adjustment of Age

Table 4.7

Sl.No	*Gender*	*N*	*A.M*	*S.D*	*M.D*	*C.R*
1.	60-69	60	23.05	1.81	4.12	14.66
2.	70&above	40	27.17	1.00		

The calculated value is 14.66 and the't 'table value is 1.98. As the table value is less than the calculated value, there is a significant difference of opinion between the age groups of 60-69 yrs and 70 and above yrs regarding the area of home aspect.

Home Adjustment of Pension

Table 4.8

Sl.No	*Gender*	*N*	*A.M*	*S.D*	*M.D*	*C.R*
1.	Pensioners	30	24.00	2.05	1.00	2.67
2.	Non-Pensioners	70	25.00		2.69	

The computed 't' value is greater than the table value. Therefore there is a considerable difference of opinions between pensioners and non-pensioners senior citizens regarding home adjustment.

Part – B: Health Adjustment of Gender

Table 4.9

Sl.No	*Gender*	*N*	*A.M*	*S.D*	*M.D*	*C.R*
1.	Male	50	25.62	3.49	0.86	1.34
2.	Female	50	24.76	2.97		

As the constructed't 'value is less than the table value, there is no significant difference between male and female regarding the health adjustment of senior citizens.

Health Adjustment of Age

Table 4.10

Sl.No	*Gender*	*N*	*A.M*	*S.D*	*M.D*	*C.R*
1.	60-69	60	27.18	2.31	4.98	11.82
2.	70&above	40	22.2	1.89		

The obtained value is 11.82 and the table value is 1.98. As the table value is less than the obtained value, there is significant difference between the senior citizens of the age groups of 60-69 and 70 and above in health problem.

Health Adjustment of Pension

Table 4.11

Sl.No	*Gender*	*N*	*A.M*	*S.D*	*M.D*	*C.R*
1.	Pensioners	30	26.33	3.16	1.63	2.39
2.	Non-Pensioners	70	24.70	3.19		

The significant value is greater than the table value, therefore null hypothesis is rejected and alternative hypothesis is accepted. There is significant difference between pensioners and non-pensioners regarding health aspect

Part-C: Social Adjustment of Gender

Table 4.12

Sl.No	*Gender*	*N*	*A.M*	*S.D*	*M.D*	*C.R*
1.	Male	50	25.38	2.94	1.18	2.31
2.	Female	50	26.56	2.26		

As the table value is less than the calculated value, therefore there is considerable difference between male and female of senior citizens in the aspects of social adjustment.

Social Adjustment of Age

Table 4.13

Sl.No	*Age*	*N*	*A.M*	*S.D*	*M.D*	*C.R*
1.	60-69	60	24.31	1.71	4.13	11.50
2.	70&above	40	28.45	1.81		

As the constructed value is greater than the table value, there is a significant difference between the age groups of 60-69 and 70 & above regarding the area of social adjustment problem.

Social Adjustment of Pension

Table 4.14

Sl.No	*Financial Support*	*N*	*A.M*	*S.D*	*M.D*	*C.R*
1.	Pensioners	30	24.66	2.61	1.62	2.94
2.	Non-pensioners	70	26.51	2.57		

The table value is less than the obtained value; there is considerable difference of opinion between pensioners and non-pensioner senior citizens in social aspect.

4.3.4 *PART-D: Emotional Adjustment of Gender*

Table 4.15

Sl.No	*Gender*	*N*	*A.M*	*S.D*	*M.D*	*C.R*
1.	Male	50	24.9	2.65	0.32	0.69
2.	Female	50	25.22	2.20		

The mathematical value is less than the table value, therefore null hypothesis is accepted and alternative hypothesis is rejected. There is no significant difference of opinion between senior citizens of male and female regarding the adjustment of emotional.

Emotional Adjustment of Age

Table 4.16

Sl.No	*Age*	*N*	*A.M*	*S.D*	*M.D*	*C.R*
1.	60-69	60	23.48	1.56	3.94	14.07
2.	70&above	40	27.42	1.33		

The significant value is greater than the table value and there is considerable difference in senior citizens between 60-60 and 70 & above age groups regarding emotional adjustment.

Emotional Adjustment of Pension

Table 4.17

Sl.No.	*Financial Support*	*N*	*A.M*	*S.D*	*M.D*	*C.R*
1.	Pensioners	30	24.66	2.44	0.56	1.09
2.	Non-Pensioners	70	25.22	2.43		

The measured value is less than the table value and therefore the alternative hypothesis is rejected and null hypothesis is accepted. And there is no significant difference between the pensioners and non-pensioner senior citizens regarding the area of emotional adjustment.

Part-E: Financial Adjustment of Gender

Table 4.18

Sl.No	*Gender*	*N*	*A.M*	*S.D*	*M.D*	*C.R*
1.	Male	50	23.8	3.66	0.24	0.40
2.	Female	50	24.04	2.33		

The computed value is less than the table value. Therefore there is no considerable difference of opinion between male and female regarding financial aspect of senior citizens.

Financial Adjustment of Age

Table 4.19

Sl.No.	*Age*	*N*	*A.M*	*S.D*	*M.D*	*C.R*
1.	60-69	60	25.43	1.81	3.78	6.88
2.	70 & above	40	21.65	3.15		

As the table value is greater than the obtained value, there is a significant difference of opinion between the age groups of 60-69 and 70 & above regarding the area of financial adjustment of senior citizens.

Financial Adjustment of Pension

Table 4.20

Sl.No.	*Financial Support*	*N*	*A.M*	*S.D*	*M.D*	*C.R*
1.	Pensioners	30	25.53	2.40	2.30	4.10
2.	Non-Pensioners	70	23.22	3.06		

The calculated 't' value is greater than the table value. Therefore the null hypothesis is rejected and alternative hypothesis is accepted. And there is considerable difference between pensioners and non-pensioners in the aspects of financial adjustment.

Graphic Representations

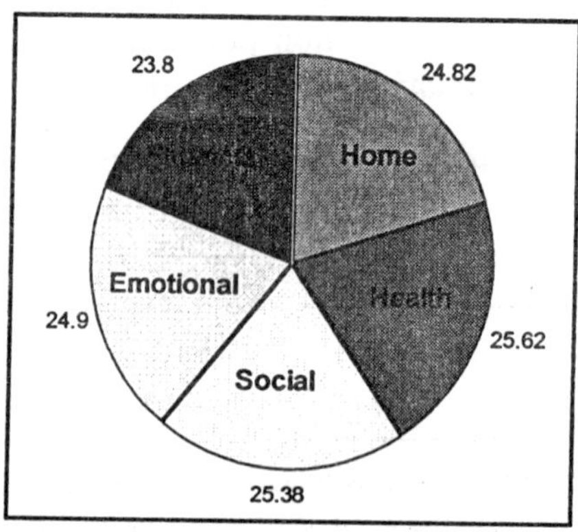

Chart 4.1. Male Average Adjustments

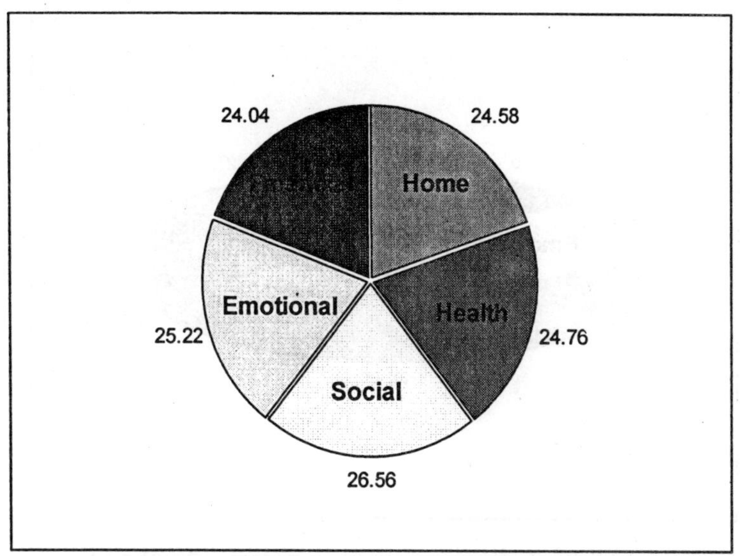

Chart 4.2. Female Average Adjustments

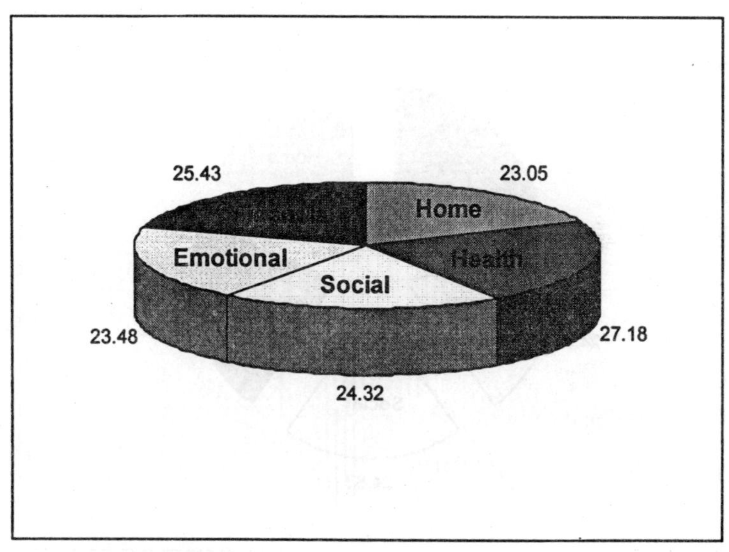

Chart 4.3. 60 – 69 yrs Age Group Average Adjustment

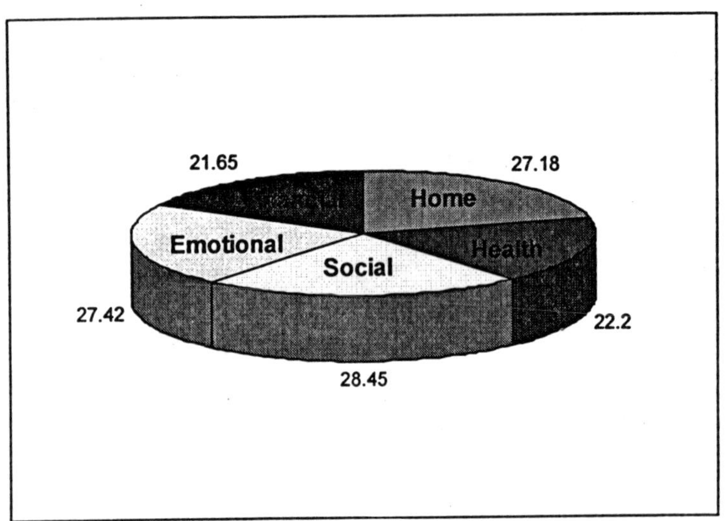

Chart 4.4. 70 & above age group average adjustments

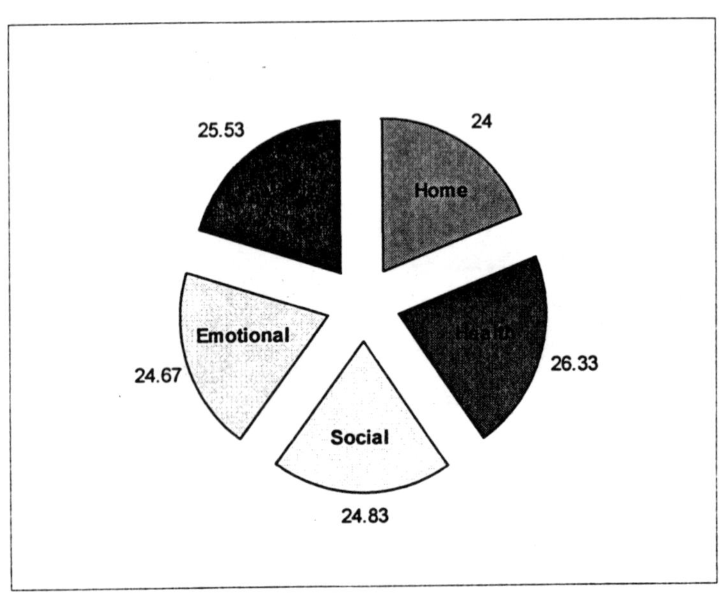

Chart 4.5. Average adjustments of pensioners group

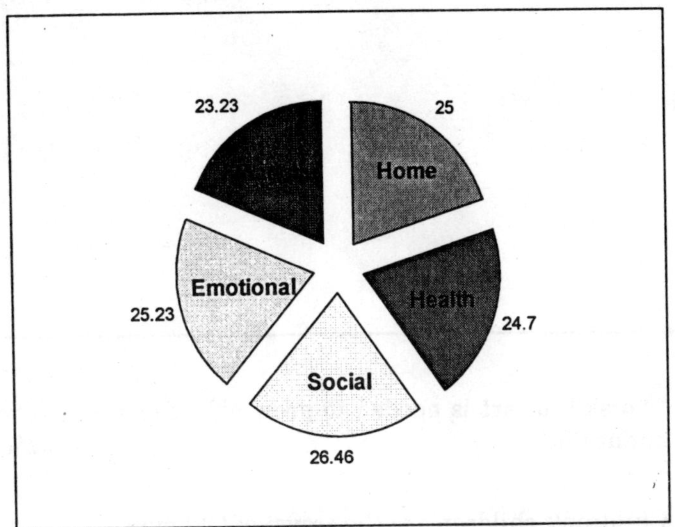

Chart 4.6. Average adjustments of non-pensioners group

Five Components of the Topic Diagram

"No skill of art is needed to grow old : the secret is to endure it."

—*Goethe*

Children's children are the crown of Old men,
And the glories of children are their fathers.

(Proverbs 17th chapter 6th verse)

5
Findings

The tool is divided into five areas of adjustment. Each area consists of 15 items with two alternative responses, 'yes / no'. The percentages of each item are mentioned below.

Home Adjustment

1. Do you feel happy at your home?

86% of senior citizens have given accepted reply for the happiness in home and 14% have given unaccepted response.

2. Do you feel more comfortable at your home without any disturbances?

87% of senior citizens have given wishful reply for the comfortable in home and 13% have given unwishful response.

3. Do you look after your own things with out others support at your home?

81% of senior citizens have given willing reply for the own things in home and 19% have given unwilling response.

4. Do you concentrate on religious aspects such as praying in your home?

85% of senior citizens have given favorable reply for the praying in home and 15% have given negative response.

5. Do you feel lonely when you are alone at home?

33% of senior citizens have given positive reply for the loneliness in home and 67% have given negative response.

6. Do you spend some time by reading Holy Books?

54% of senior citizens have given favorable reply for the

reading holy books in home and 46% have given unfavorable response.

7. Do you spend some time in reading newspaper or magazines at your home?

46% of senior citizens have given favorable reply for the reading news papers in home and 54% have given unfavorable response.

8. Do you enjoy the leisure time by watching TV?

39% of senior citizens have given positive reply for the watching T.V in home and 61% have given negative response.

9. Do you enjoy favourable music at your home?

45% of senior citizens have given accepted reply for the music in home and 55% have given unaccepted response.

10. Do you spend some time in gardening work at your home?

60% of senior citizens have given willing reply for the gardening work in home and 40% have given negative response.

11. Do you enjoy with your grand children at home?

77% of senior citizens have given wishful reply for the grand children in home and 23% have given un-wishful response.

12. Do you satisfy with care and affection shown by your family members?

80% of senior citizens have given positive reply for the care and affection in home and 20% have given negative response.

13. Do other friends or relatives of your age will visit you at home?

69% of senior citizens have given favorable reply for the friends visit in home and 31% have given unfavorable response.

14. Do you spend some time in letter correspondence at your home?

48% of senior citizens have given favorable reply for the letter correspondence in home and 52% have given unfavorable response.

15. Do you feel secure with strangers when you are at home?

80% of senior citizens have given positive reply for the security in home and 20% have given negative response.

Health Adjustment

1. Do you feel happy with your health?

80% of senior citizens have given favorable reply for the happiness about health and 20% have given unfavorable response.

2. Do you have any problem with your sight?

72% of senior citizens have given accepted reply for the problem with sight and 28% have given unaccepted response.

3. Do you suffer from joint pains?

59% of senior citizens have given willing reply for the joint pains and 41% have given unwilling response.

4. Do you usually feel exhausted?

59% of senior citizens have given positive reply for the tiredness and 41% have given negative response.

5. Are you usually anxious about your health?

64% of senior citizens have given accepted reply for the anxiety about health and 36% have given unaccepted response.

6. Do you take any care for your diet?

46% of senior citizens have given willing reply for the care for diet and 54% have given unwilling response.

7. Do you feel difficult at sleeping during nights?

70% of senior citizens have given favorable reply for the difficulty of sleep and 30% have given unfavorable response.

8. Do you keep on changing sides for a long time while lying on bed?

68% of senior citizens have given accepted reply for the changing sides for a long time on bed and 32% have given unaccepted response.

9. Do you suffer from B.P?

62% of senior citizens have given wishful reply for the B.P and 38% have given un-wishful response.

10. Do you suffer from sugar?

61% of senior citizens have given willing reply for the sugar and 39% have given unwilling response.

11. Do you use long medication?

63% of senior citizens have given favorable reply for the long medication and 37% have given unfavorable response.

12. Do you visit doctor regularly?

69% of senior citizens have given positive reply for the doctor visits and 31% have given negative response.

13. Do you smoke?

85% of senior citizens have given favorable reply for the smoking and 15% have given unfavorable response.

14. Do you take any alcohol?

86% of senior citizens have given positive reply for the usage of alcohol and 14% have given negative response.

15. Are you doing walking exercises?

53% of senior citizens have given accepted reply for the walking exercise and 47% have given unaccepted response.

Social Adjustment

1. Do you spend with your grand children?

81% of senior citizens have given willing reply for the spending with grand children and 19% has given unwilling response.

2. Do you share your pervious experiences with your children / grand children when ever necessary?

80% of senior citizens have given positive reply for the sharing of previous experiences with children and 20% have given negative response.

3. Do you maintain friendly relationship with all?

90% of senior citizens have given accepted reply for the friendly relationship and 10% have given unaccepted response.

4. Do you usually get irritated on the members of your family?

82% of senior citizens have given willing reply for the irritation on family and 18% have given unwilling response.

5. Do you usually have trouble in recognizing people?

78% of senior citizens have given wishful reply for the recognizing people and 22% have given un-wishful response.

6. Do your friends or relatives will visit you?

77% of senior citizens have given positive reply for the relatives visit and 23% have given negative response.

7. Do you visit your friends or relatives of their houses?

67% of senior citizens have given favorable reply for the visit to friends and relatives, and 33% have given unfavorable response.

8. Do you spend some time with your neighbors?

72% of senior citizens have given accepted reply for the spending with neighbors and 28% have given unaccepted response.

9. Are you troubled when you have different opinions on others?

83% of senior citizens have given willing reply for the troubling with different opinions and 17% have given unwilling response.

10. Do your heart is hurt by the small things of others?

79% of senior citizens have given wishful reply for the things of others and 21% have given unwishful response.

11. Do people usually think you to be a useless man?

92% of senior citizens have given positive reply for the people's opinion and only 8% have given negative response.

12. Do you visit your religious society?

66% of senior citizens have given favorable reply for the religious society and 34% have given unfavorable response.

13. Do you have any gathering for recreation in the evening?

58% of senior citizens have given accepted reply for the recreation and 42% have given unaccepted response.

14. Do you visit your children homes far away or in abroad?

44% of senior citizens have given willing reply for the visit to children and 56% have given unwilling response.

15. Do you travel to visit pilgrimage?

48% of senior citizens have given wishful reply for the pilgrimage and 52% have given un-wishful response.

Emotional Adjustment

1. Do you feel happy with your children/grand children?

80% of senior citizens have given positive reply for the happiness about children and 20% have given negative response.

2. Do you take care of your children/grand children?

74% of senior citizens have given favourable reply for the care about children and 26% have given unfavorable response.

3. Do you like your friends/relatives?

67% of senior citizens have given favorable reply for the happiness in home. 33% have given negative response.

4. Do you like the presence of your neighbors?

85% of senior citizens have given accepted reply for the presence of neighbors and 15% have given unaccepted response.

5. Do you affectionate with others of your age?

94% of senior citizens have given willing reply for the affection on others and only 6% have given unwilling response.

6. Do you feel any anxiety or tension?

76% of senior citizens have given wishful reply for the tension and 24% have given un-wishful response.

7. Do you get anger easily or quickly?

77% of senior citizens have given positive reply for the anger and 23% have given negative response.

8. Do you get excited soon?

73% of senior citizens have given favourable reply for the excitement and 27% have given unfavorable response.

9. Do you cry very soon?

56% of senior citizens have given accepted reply for the crying and 44% have given unaccepted response.

10. Are you often disturbed of the fearful dreams?

52% of senior citizens have given willing reply for the fearful dreams and 48% have given unwilling response.

11. Do you feel fear by seeing quarrel?

47% of senior citizens have given wishful reply for the seeing quarrel and 53% have given un-wishful response.

12. Do you feel that some trouble is ahead?

75% of senior citizens have given positive reply for the troubles and 25% have given negative response.

13. Do you keep on thinking about your past?

47% of senior citizens have given favorable reply for the thinking about past and 53% has given unfavorable response.

14. Do you get irritated in your home?

54% of senior citizens have given accepted reply for the irritation in home and 46% have given unaccepted response.

15. Do you get disturbed with your children / grand children?

49% of senior citizens have given willing reply for the disturbance with children and 51% have given unwilling response.

Financial Adjustment

1. Do you get pension?

30% of senior citizens have given wishful reply for the pension and 70% have given un-wishful response.

2. Do you satisfy with the money you get?

83% of senior citizens have given positive reply for the money and 17% have given negative response.

3. Do you get any money from business?

37% of senior citizens have given favorable reply for the business and 63% have given unfavorable response.

4. Do you get money from fields / cattle?

27% of senior citizens have given accepted reply for the money from fields and 73% have given unaccepted response.

5. Do you get rent from your own house?

61% of senior citizens have given willing reply for rent and 39% have given unwilling response.

6. Do you have any fixed deposits?

48% of senior citizens have given wishful reply for the fixed deposits and 52% have given un-wishful response.

7. Do you pay any income tax for your assets?

Only 3% of senior citizens have given positive reply for the income tax and 97% have given negative response.

8. Do you have any financial problems?

63% of senior citizens have given favorable reply for the financial problems and 37% have given unfavorable response.

9. Do you face any problem by your family members because of financial aspects?

74% of senior citizens have given accepted reply for the problems by family and 26% have given unaccepted response.

10. Do you take any loan from bank or others?

39% of senior citizens have given willing reply for the bank loan and 61% have given unwilling response.

11. Do you spend your money to your children/grand children?

93% of senior citizens have given wishful reply for the spending money and only 7% have given un-wishful response.

12. Do you support any religious/social organization?

79% of senior citizens have given positive reply for the supporting organizations and 21% have given negative response.

13. Do you spend money in a planned way?

88% of senior citizens have given favorable reply for the spending money and 12% have given unfavorable response.

14. Do you feel that the expenditure is more at your home?

71% of senior citizens have given accepted reply for the expenditure and 29% have given unaccepted response.

15. Do you repay the amounts which you have taken from other?

96% of senior citizens have given willing reply for the repayment and only 4% have given unwilling response.

Now also when I am old and gray headed, O God, forsake me not; until I have shewed thy strength unto this generation, and thy power to every one that is to come.

(Psalms 71st chapter 18th verse)

Do not sharply rebuke on older man, but rather appeal to him as a father, the older women as mothers.

(1 Timothy 5th chapter 1st and 2nd verses)

6

Conclusions and Suggestions

The present study consists of five areas of adjustment. Based on these adjustments, the conclusions were framed.

Any recommendation, as to the application of the findings, the researcher wishes to make, can find a place in this chapter. Recommendations or suggestions for further study in the field are also found useful and are usually included in the concluding chapter.

To derive, verified and verifiable conclusions, an educational research worker has to exercise all care and caution in formulating conclusions and generalizations on the basis of the data. The interpretation of results and the formulation of conclusions and generalizations demand keen observation, wide out look and power of logical thinking.

Home Adjustment

1. **Gender:** Since the critical ratio value is not significant at 0.05 levels, and there is no considerable difference between the opinions, of male and female regarding home adjustment.

   Since male senior citizens engage in so many activities in home, where as female senior citizens mostly engaged in household work and cooking. Therefore, both male and female expressed almost equal opinions about home adjustment.

2. **Age:** Since the critical ratio value is significant at 0.05 levels and there is a considerable difference between the opinions, of 60-69 yr and 70 & above yr age groups regarding the impact of home adjustment.

Since 60-69 yr age group is some what energetic and they are capable to do the household work outside the home. But 70 & above senior citizens mostly spend in home. Therefore these two groups expressed different opinions about the home adjustment.

3. **Financial Support:** Since the critical ratio value is not significant at 0.05 levels and there is a considerable difference between the opinions, of pensioners and non-pensioners groups regarding the home adjustment.

   Since the home environment is more comfortable to pensioners, so that, they are getting money and non-pensioners are not. So, both these groups have expressed different opinions on home adjustment.

Health Adjustment

1. **Gender:** Since the critical ration value is not significant at 0.05 levels and there is no considerable variation between the opinions, of male and female senior citizens regarding health adjustment.

   Since the senior citizens are having naturally and normally some physical problems like weakness, sight problem, joint pains, etc. These are all common after 60 yrs of age. So, there is no considerable difference between, male and female regarding health adjustment.

2. **Age:** Since the critical ratio value is significant at 0.05 levels and there is considerable variation between, 60-69 yr and 70 & above yrs senior citizens on health adjustment.

   Since the age gap between 60-69 and 70 & above groups is ten years so that, there is lot of difference in relationship with health aspects of the senior citizens. So, both the groups differ in the opinions in the aspects of health.

3. **Financial Support:** Since the critical ratio value is significant at 0.05 levels and there is considerable difference between, pensioners and non-pensioners groups about health adjustment.

Since the pensioners group can spend money about their health in medical aspects so that, there is a considerable difference between the opinions, of these two groups regarding health adjustment.

Social Adjustment

1. **Gender:** Since the critical ratio value is significant at 0.05 levels and there is a considerable variation between the opinions, of male and female senior citizens regarding social adjustment.

   Since the male senior citizens spend much time in social aspects. Female senior citizens spend much time in home and they have less time to build social relationships compare to men. So, there is a difference between the opinions, of male and female senior citizens regarding social adjustment.

2. **Age:** Since the critical ratio value is significant at 0.05 levels and there is a difference between the opinions, of 60-69 yr and 70 & above yr *senior citizens regarding* social adjustment.

   Since the 60-69 yrs the age group senior citizens are capable to build up social relationships but, 70 & above yr senior citizens can not build up that much social relationships. So, here both the groups differ in the aspects of social adjustment.

3. **Financial Support:** Since the critical ratio value is significant at 0.05 levels and there s a variation between the opinions, of pensioners and non-pensioners regarding the social adjustment.

   Since the pensioners group can afford some money to build social relationship but, the non-pensioners group can not afford that much money. So, here both the groups expressed different opinions about the social adjustment.

Emotional Adjustment

1. **Gender:** Since the critical ratio value is not significant at 0.05 levels and there is no considerable difference

between the opinions, of male and female senior citizens regarding emotional adjustment.

Since the male and female senior citizens are having both equal emotions so that, both are human beings. Therefore there is no difference between the opinions, of male and female senior citizens regarding emotional adjustment.

2. **Age:** Since the critical ratio value is significant at 0.05 levels and there is a considerable difference between the opinions, of 60-69 yr and 70 & above yr regarding the emotional adjustment.

   Since 60-69 yrs senior citizens, there is a possibility of excitement, anxiety, tension about their problems and worries in their mind. But, 70 & above yr senior citizens are low in excitement of emotions. So, there is a difference between these two groups in emotional adjustment.

3. **Financial Support:** Since the critical ratio value is not significant at 0.05 levels and there is no difference between the opinions, of pensioners and non-pensioner senior citizens regarding emotional adjustment.

   Since the emotions are common factors for the people so that, there is no considerable difference between the opinions of pensioners and non-pensioner groups regarding emotional adjustment.

Financial Adjustment

1. **Gender:** Since the critical ratio value is not significant at 0.05 levels and there is no considerable difference between the opinions, of male and female senior citizens in the aspects of financial adjustment.

   Since the male expenditure is vary with female expenditure so, there is no considerable variation of expenditure either male or female senior citizens regarding the aspects of financial adjustment.

2. **Age:** Since the critical ratio value is significant at 0.05 levels and there is a considerable difference between

the opinions, of 60-69 yr and 70 & above yr senior citizens regarding financial adjustment.

Since 60-69 yr can spend money in a planned way. They are energetic and have strength to deal with financial matters. Where as 70 yr & above senior citizens are weak and lean and can not deal with the money matters. So, both the groups expressed the different opinions about financial adjustment.

3. **Financial Support:** Since critical ratio value is significant at 0.05 levels and there is a considerable variation between the opinions, of pensioners and non-pensioner senior citizens regarding financial adjustment.

   Since the pensioners get pension and they need not worry about their money. They will spend money to children and also some organizations. But for non-pensioners group, they face some financial problems. So, there is a considerable difference between these two groups in the aspects of financial adjustment.

Suggestions

Some objective suggestions were attempted to be given here under. These suggestions follow the main conclusions of major importance. Each suggestion is followed by logical discussions where ever necessary regarding the findings concluded basing on which the suggestions were given.

Home Adjustment

The critical ratio value about the variable gender is not significant at 0.05 levels. It indicates that there is no difference in the opinions of male and female in home adjustment. But age and pension are significant at 0.05 levels. It indicates that there is a difference between 60-69 yr and 70 & above yr, pensioners and non-pensioner senior citizens in the aspects of home adjustment.

Male senior citizens engage in so many activities in home, where as female senior citizens mostly engaged in household work and cooking. Therefore both the groups expressed equal opinions and there is no considerable difference.

Since 60-69 yrs age group is some what energetic and they are capable to do the household work outside the home. But 70 & above senior citizens mostly spend in home. Therefore these two groups expressed different opinions of the home adjustment.

Since the home environment is more comfortable to pensioners, so that, they are getting money and non-pensioner are not. So, both these groups have expressed different opinions on home adjustment.

Health Adjustment

The critical ratio value for gender is not significant at 0.05 levels. So there is no difference of opinions about health between male and female. The critical ratio value of age and pension of health adjustment are significant at 0.05 levels. So there is a difference between 60-69 and 70 & above in health aspects, and there is difference between pensioners and non-pensioner groups related to health adjustment.

Since the senior citizens are having naturally and normally some physical problems like weakness, sight problem, joint pains, etc. These are all common after 60 yr of age. So, there is no considerable difference between male and female regarding health adjustment.

Concern to age the gap between 60-69 and 70 & above groups is ten years. So, there is lot of difference in relationship with health aspects of the senior citizens. So, both the groups differ in the opinions in the aspects of health.

The pensioners group can spend money about their health in medical aspects. So, there is a considerable difference between the opinions of pensioners and non-pensioner groups.

Social Adjustment

Critical ratio values about the variables gender, age and pension of senior citizens are significant at 0.05 levels. It indicates that there is considerable difference in the opinions between male and female, the age groups of 60-69 yr and 70 & above yr and pensioners and non-pensioners.

The male senior citizens spend much time in social aspects. Female senior citizens spend much time in home and thy have less time to build social relationships compare to men. So, there is a difference between the opinions of male and female senior citizens regarding social adjustment.

Since the 60-69 yr the age group senior citizens are capable to build up social relationships but, 70 & above yr senior citizens can not build up that much social relationships. So, both the groups differ in the aspects of social adjustment.

The pensioners group can afford some money to build social relationships but, the non-pensioner group can not afford that much money. So, both the groups expressed different opinions about the social adjustment.

Emotional Adjustment

The critical ratio values for gender and pension is not significant at 0.05 levels. Therefore there is no difference of opinions about emotional adjustment between male and female and pensioners and non-pensioners. But the critical ratio value of age is significant at 0.05 level, it indicates that, there is a difference between 60-69 and 70 & above senior citizens regarding emotional adjustment.

Since the male and female senior citizens are having both equal emotions so that, both are human beings. Therefore there is no difference between the opinions of male and female senior citizens regarding emotional adjustment.

60-69 yr senior citizens, there is a possibility of excitement, anxiety, tension about their problems and worries in their mind. But, 70 & above yrs senior citizens are low in excitement of emotions. So, there is a difference between these two groups in emotional adjustment.

Since the emotions are common factors for the people so that, there is no considerable difference between the opinions of pensioners and non-pensioner groups in the aspects of emotional adjustment.

Financial Adjustment

Critical ratio value of gender is not significant at 0.05 levels. So there is no difference of opinions between male and female regarding financial aspects of senor citizens. But age and pension are significant at 0.05 levels. It indicates that there is a difference between 60-69 yr/70 & above yrs, and pensioners and non-pensioner senior citizens in the aspects of financial adjustment.

Since the male expenditure is vary with female expenditure but, the amount of expenditure is same for both. So, there is no considerable variation of expenditure either male or female senior citizens regarding the aspects of financial adjustment.

Concern to the age groups of 60-69 yr can spend money in a planned way. They are energetic and have strength to deal with financial matters. Where as 70 yr & above senior citizens are weak and lean and can not deal with the money matters. So, both the groups expressed the different opinions about financial adjustment.

Since the pensioners get pension and they need not worry about their money. They will spend money to children and also some organizations. But for non-pensioner group, they face some financial problems. So, there is a considerable difference between these two groups in the aspects of financial adjustment.

Bibliography

Bhatia, H.R. (1965), *Elements of Social Psychology.* Bombay, Manaktalas.

Elizabeth, B. Hurlock, (2005), *Developmental Psychology: A Life Span Approach*, New Delhi: Tata McGraw-Hill Publishing Company Limited.

Good, C.V. (1945). *Dictionary of Education.* New York: McGraw-Hill Book co., Inc.

John, Keats (1901), *The Poetical Works of John Keats. World's Classics,* London: Oxford University, and Press Humphrey Milford.

Lazarus, R.S. (1976), *Patterns of Adjustment.* Tokyo, McGraw-Hill Kogakusha Pvt. Ltd.

Lindgren, H.C. (1959). *Psychology of Personal and Social Adjustment,* (2nd). New York: American Book Company.

Hima, Bindu. (2005), Problems of Senior Citizens M.Ed. dissertation, St. Joseph's College of Education for Women, Guntur.

New American Standard Bible, (1976), (psalms 90th chapter 10th verse), Study Edition, Philadelphia, A.J. Holman Company.

Ruch, F.L. (1970), *Psychology and Life.* Bombay: D. B. Taraporewala Sons and Co.

Shaffer, G.W and Lazarus, R.S. (1952). *Fundamental Concepts in Clinical Psychology.* New York: McGraw-Hill.

Shaffer, L.F and Shoben, E.J. (1956). *The Psychology of Adjustment.* Boston: Houghton Mifflin Co.

Smith, H.C. (1961). *Personality Adjustment.* New York: McGraw-Hill Book Co.

William Shakespeare. (1978), *All the World's a stage. Realms of Gold, an anthology of poems,* S. Chand & Company Limited.

Index

❑❑❑